OCEANS ALIVE

Corals

by Ann Herriges

BLASTOFF!
2
READERS

BELLWETHER MEDIA • MINNEAPOLIS, MN

Note to Librarians, Teachers, and Parents:

Blastoff! Readers are carefully developed by literacy experts and combine standards-based content with developmentally appropriate text.

Level 1 provides the most support through repetition of high-frequency words, light text, predictable sentence patterns, and strong visual support.

Level 2 offers early readers a bit more challenge through varied simple sentences, increased text load, and less repetition of high-frequency words.

Level 3 advances early-fluent readers toward fluency through increased text and concept load, less reliance on visuals, longer sentences, and more literary language.

Whichever book is right for your reader, Blastoff! Readers are the perfect books to build confidence and encourage a love of reading that will last a lifetime!

This edition first published in 2007 by Bellwether Media.

No part of this publication may be reproduced in whole or in part without written permission of the publisher. For information regarding permission, write to Bellwether Media Inc., Attention: Permissions Department, Post Office Box 1C, Minnetonka, MN 55345-9998.

Library of Congress Cataloging-in-Publication Data
Herriges, Ann.
  Corals / by Ann Herriges.
     p. cm. — (Blastoff! readers) (Oceans alive!)
Summary: "Simple text and supportive images introduce beginning readers to corals. Intended for students in kindergarten through third grade."
  Includes bibliographical references and index.
  ISBN-10: 1-60014-049-1 (hardcover : alk. paper)
  ISBN-13: 978-1-60014-049-5 (hardcover : alk. paper)
  1. Corals—Juvenile literature. I. Title. II. Series. III. Series: Herriges, Ann. Oceans alive!

QL377.C5H46 2006
593.6—dc22   2006009512

Text copyright © 2007 by Bellwether Media.
Printed in the United States of America.

Table of Contents

Corals live in warm,
shallow parts of the ocean.

Sunlight shines through the shallow water. Sunlight helps corals grow.

Corals look like plants or rocks. But corals are really animals.

Corals can be very colorful.

Most corals grow in a group
called a **colony**.

Colonies grow in different shapes.

A coral's body is shaped
like a tube.

mouth

A coral has a mouth at the
top end of its body.

Small arms grow around a coral's mouth. The arms are called **tentacles**.

A coral uses its tentacles to catch food. The tentacles can sting **prey**.

A coral eats small sea animals that float in the water. It also eats small fish.

Tiny plants called **algae**
live inside a coral. The algae
make food for the coral.

15

Some corals make
coral reefs.

Each coral builds a hard **skeleton** around the bottom of its body.

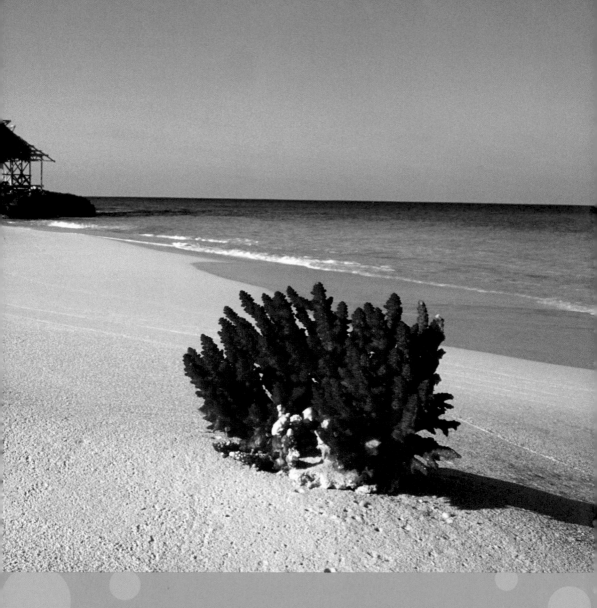

The skeleton is left behind
when a coral dies.

The skeletons build up on top of each other. The coral reef grows bigger and bigger.

Some coral reefs have been growing for thousands of years.

Many different animals live on a coral reef. Coral reefs are like cities in the ocean!

Glossary

algae—small plants that do not have roots or stems; algae grow in water.

colony—a large group of animals that live together; a coral colony can have millions of corals.

coral reef—a structure in the ocean made of the skeletons of corals; live corals live on the outside of a coral reef.

prey—an animal that is hunted by another animal for food

shallow—not deep; corals need clear, shallow water to live.

skeleton—a hard structure that supports and protects a body; some corals have a cup-shaped skeleton that they can hide in.

tentacles—the arms of some animals that are used for grabbing; a coral uses its tentacles to bring food to its mouth.

To Learn More

AT THE LIBRARY

Earle, Sylvia. *Coral Reefs*. Washington, D.C.:
National Geographic, 2003.

Lindeen, Carol K. *Corals*. Mankato, Minn.: Pebble
Books, 2005.

Muzik, Katy. *At Home in the Coral Reef*. Watertown,
Mass.: Charlesbridge, 1992.

Silver, Donald M. *Coral Reef*. New York: Learning
Triangle Press, 1998.

Stone, Lynn M. *Corals*. Vero Beach, Fla.: Rourke,
2003.

ON THE WEB

Learning more about corals
is as easy as 1, 2, 3.

1. Go to www.factsurfer.com

2. Enter "corals" into search box.

3. Click the "Surf" button and you will see a list of
   related web sites.

With factsurfer.com, finding more information is just a
click away.

Index

The photographs in this book are reproduced through the courtesy of: Bavaria/Getty Images, front cover; Joshua Singer/Getty Images pp. 4-5; altrendo nature/Getty Images, pp. 6-7; altrendo nature/Getty Images, pp. 8-9; Robert W. Madden/Getty Images, pp. 10-11; C. Wolcott Henry, III/Getty Images, p. 12; Jeff Rotman/Getty Images, p. 13; Jeffery L. Rotman/Getty Images, pp. 14-15; Louise Murray/Getty Images, p. 16; A. Witt/C. Mahaney/Getty Images, p. 17; Angelo Cavalli/Getty Images, p. 18; David Nardini/Getty Images, p. 19; Kim Westerskov/GettyImages, p. 20; Georgette Douwma/Getty Images, p. 21.